Weather
Facts and Fun

Weather
Facts and Fun

Written by **Josh Judge** and **Kathe Cussen**

Foreword by Richard Lederer
Edited by Nikki Andrews

SciArt Media
Where science meets art...

Published by SciArt Media
www.SciArtMedia.com

Praise for *Weather Facts and Fun*

"A delightful read. If you have kids or grand kids this is the book to get them. Not only will they have fun but they'll learn a lot as well. Everyone talks about the weather. This will guarantee some really neat conversations. I give Josh and Kathe's book 'five snowflakes!'"
Fritz Wetherbee
NH Author and TV Personality

"Wonderful for teachers and young students... Written in an easy to understand way that will encourage, cultivate and nurture one's interest in weather... Hands-on experiments and an accompanying interactive website add to the fun and education... Nicely done!"
Harvey Leonard
Chief Meteorologist, WCVB-TV

"We live at the bottom of a sea of air – the atmosphere – where weather brews a mix of awe, impacts and insights. There is much to discover during our daily forays in this greatest show OFF Earth, and this book is an excellent invitation to look up and learn."
Bruce Schwoegler
WBZ Meteorologist

"For curious kids, this book is the happiest weather-related development since the invention of the snow day!"
John Clayton
Writer and NH Union Leader Columnist

"Growing up in New Hampshire, our house always came to a standstill whenever the weather report came on the TV. I wish I had this marvelous book to decode and understand the forecast. I would have been better enabled to predict snow-days and skip my homework for the night."
Dr. James Collins
Distinguished Professor, B.U., Rhodes Scholar, MacArthur Genius

"Weather Facts and Fun certainly is fun! A great introduction to weather for elementary school students. From cloud types to tornadoes, all topics are covered in a way that 7-11 year olds will clearly understand."
Mike Haddad
WMUR Meteorologist

Table of Contents

PREFACE

The weather is all around you and is something that everyone in the world notices and talks about all the time. Hopefully this book will give you a new way to look at the weather and perhaps understand it a little bit more. We think that after reading this book, you'll look at the sky in new ways and will see how wonderful and amazing it can be.

The writers of this book have tried to find new and fun ways to explain the weather, and even show you things not often mentioned in other such books! There are pictures, experiments and activities. At the end of the book are maps so that you can track and follow the weather like real meteorologists do (but make sure you read the book to learn how to use them!)

Special thanks to WMUR-TV for their support of this book.

Josh would like to thank his wife, Donna, for her support and encouragement.

Thanks to the National Weather Service and The National Oceanic and Atmospheric Administration for the use of some of their great pictures you'll see on upcoming pages.

Kathe would like to thank her daughter, Kerry, for her assistance with the cover and charts.

There are links to many weather resources at our website: www.weatherfactsandfun.com.

Thanks for reading, and please let us know your comments or questions about the book or weather in general, using the e-mail provided at our website.

FOREWORD

Have you ever noticed how much our thoughts and our language reflect the weather? Certain people strike us as stuffy, chilly, cool, cold, icy, or frigid, while others seem to radiate a warm and sunny disposition. Because temperature, moisture, and wind conditions are so important in our lives, a variety of weather patterns blow hot and cold through many of the descriptive phrases in our speech and writing.

I'm confident that this book will not make you feel that you're under the weather, a common expression that comes to us from the language of sailors. On the high seas when the wind starts to blow hard and the water becomes rough, crewmen and travelers go below deck and down to their cabins in order to ride out the storm and avoid becoming seasick. In this way they literally retreat to a location "under the weather."

The authors didn't write this book about weather just to shoot the breeze, create a tempest in a teapot, or steal your thunder. They didn't try to barnstorm through the topic and take you on a whirlwind tour that would leave you in a fog. Rather, the information in the pages you are about to read will come to you like a bolt from the blue. As you brainstorm the facts, you'll be on cloud nine and occasionally experience gales of laughter. They've created a great climate for learning.

So don't take a rain check. It's time to break the ice and learn about something that is with you all the time - the weather.

Richard Lederer
Author, Educator,
Former PBS Host

Chapter 1:

People who Study and Predict the Weather

There are many types of scientists, and those who observe and forecast the weather are known as meteorologists. Why are they called this? After all, they study the weather and not meteors up in space! The word is very old, and comes from the ancient Greek word, "Meteorologica," which means "things that fall from the sky." Meteorologists use science and math in their job every day, and also spend a lot of time watching and thinking about the weather.

There are many types of meteorologists, but you've probably heard about or seen the kind on TV. They stand in front of maps showing what the weather is doing now, and what it will do in the future.

Josh Judge, one of the authors of this book, gives a weather forecast for New Hampshire on television. This is how he appears on screen to viewers at home.

You wake up in the morning and want to know what kind of clothes you should wear. Your parents might watch the weather to see if they need to take an umbrella to work, or if they can mow the lawn or play sports outside. Maybe you're wondering if there will be school the next morning. We all need to know what the weather will be, and television meteorologists help us figure that out.

A TV weather person is someone who went to school for many years to understand how weather works. Every day TV weather people look at hundreds of maps, temperatures, and numbers to figure out what will happen next. They study satellite and radar pictures (We'll talk about those in chapter 4) to help them know where it is raining, snowing, cloudy, or sunny. They also check weather reports from people all over the area so they know what kind of weather is happening all around them.

Then the forecasters stand in front of a blank blue or green wall and *pretend* to point at maps with the weather charts on them. They *pretend* because they aren't really standing in front of a map, and they are actually pointing at *nothing!* Computers put maps of clouds, temperatures, rain and more on the blank screen behind the meteorologists. They watch themselves on a TV to see what they are pointing at while they talk. (See pictures.) For this job, you need to be good at speaking very clearly and explaining the weather so that people watching TV can understand.

Josh in front of the blank wall at WMUR-TV in Manchester. Notice how you see nothing behind him, yet when you watch on TV, you see the maps.

There is a TV to the side of the blank wall, so that when Josh turns and "looks" at the maps behind him, he is really looking at the TV so he can see what he is pointing at!

A television meteorologist works some very strange times of day and night so that people just waking up or going to bed can watch the news and weather. Most of the time weather people get up in the middle of the night or stay up very late to do their job. It can also be a very fun career, as you tell people about exciting changes that are about to occur in the weather.

Meteorologists do more than just work on TV. They also:

- Work as researchers who study weather patterns so we can forecast better.
- Predict weather for airlines so that the planes know where to fly to avoid storms and bumpy rides.
- Forecast strong storms and issue special warnings.
- Work for the weather agencies like the National Weather Service.
- Teach weather in schools and colleges.
- Forecast for oil rigs out in the ocean so they know when a storm or rough seas are coming in.
- Predict the weather just for radio stations or internet websites.

Most people who become meteorologists go to college for four years and study a lot of math and science.

Weather
FACT

CHAPTER CHALLENGES

1) Be a meteorologist! Look at a map or globe and pick a country. Go online and find out what tomorrow's weather will be there. Write and perform a simple "live" forecast.

2) The word "meteorologist" means a "scientist who studies things that fall from the sky." What do these other scientists study: biologist? geologist? ecologist? How about these hard ones: limnologist? herpetologist? entomologist? Check out this web site for more types of scientists: http://phrontistery.info/sciences.html

Chapter 2:

How Weather Affects Your Life

The weather is very important because it affects every single living thing on Earth. It determines what kind of things you can do outside. If it's raining or too cold or hot, you might not have outdoor recess. When it snows, you can go sledding or skiing. When it's sunny, you can play sports or just sit outside and relax. Rainy

"A Windy Day"
By Jolie Nadeau
Teacher: Ms. Cummings
Hampstead Middle School

days can make you want to stay inside and can even ruin outdoor fun like picnics, birthday parties, and other big events.

But imagine if there was no rain. What would happen? Flowers, grass, and other plant life would dry up and die.

Animals and people also need water to survive and rain is the biggest way we get our supply.

Of course, TOO much rain can lead to floods and *nobody* likes those. Sometimes clouds keep bringing too much rain, and the ground, lakes, and rivers can't hold any more water. When this happens, water starts to do things it shouldn't, like pouring into your house or covering up roads.

May 2006, Spring flooding in Salem, New Hampshire. A road is completely covered in water. When this happens, it is very dangerous to drive through, as the water can carry the car away.

Weather affects us in many other ways as well. If it's a very hot day, you may need to go inside where there's cool air conditioning, or go swimming. You also wear lighter clothes like shorts and short sleeve shirts.

How high has the temperature risen?
Taylor C., Hampstead Middle School,
Hampstead, NH

The highest and lowest temperatures EVER for New England in degrees Fahrenheit

HOTTEST			COLDEST		

New Hampshire

| 106° | 7/4/1911 | Nashua | -47° | 1/29/1934 | Mount Washington |

Maine

| 105° | 7/10/1911 | N. Bridgton | -50° | 1/16/2009 | Big Black River |

Vermont

| 105° | 7/4/1911 | Vernon | -50° | 12/30/1933 | Bloomfield |

Massachusetts

| 107° | 8/2/1975 | New Bedford | -35° | 1/12/1981 | Chester |

Connecticut

| 106° | 7/15/1995 | Danbury | -32° | 2/16/1943 | Falls Village |

Rhode Island

| 104° | 8/2/1975 | Providence | -25° | 2/5/1996 | Greene |

In the summertime, it is sometimes very humid. When water is an invisible gas in the air that we can't see but we can feel, it's called *water vapor*. When it is humid, there is a lot more water vapor in the air. Humid weather makes us feel hotter and sometimes more uncomfortable. It can also make you sweat more when you exercise. Some people hate hot and humid weather and some people love it. How about you?

When it's cold you wear heavy coats, scarves, and mittens. When it's snowing it can be very hard to drive. Even when the roads have been plowed, they can still be slippery. Streets covered with rain or ice are also dangerous.

Driving in snow is hard to do and sometimes can be dangerous. That's why schools are closed in bad snowstorms, because roads can be very slippery.

You can see how weather is so important! It determines what we wear, where we go, how we get there, and what we do. Some people enjoy hot weather and some people don't. Some people love summer the most, others think winter is the best. Which is your favorite?

Weather
FACT

The wind can also be a big part of how the weather feels to you. On a hot summer day, a nice wind can cool you off and make you feel comfortable. On a cold winter day, wind can feel extremely cold. Your body makes heat to keep you warm. When there are parts of your body not covered up, like your hands and head, the wind blows that body heat away from you so you feel colder. This is called the *wind chill factor.*

CLOUDS

Cumulus Clouds over Concord, NH

Don't they look a lot like giant cotton balls or cotton candy? These clouds can be quite pretty. Sometimes you may look at them and think they look like an object, an animal, or just about anything!

Cumulus clouds often form on nicer days with fair weather, so many people also call them "fair weather clouds."

Stratus Clouds - Over Lake Winnipesaukee, NH

These clouds have no real shape as they are mostly flat. They are like a giant blanket that sometimes covers the sun and sky. They may be thin enough for the sun to shine through just a bit or, as in this picture, they don't cover the whole sky so it is still a nice day. These clouds sometimes move in before rainy or snowy weather arrives.

Nimbostratus Clouds over Hampstead, NH

These are a lot like stratus clouds, except they can be much thicker and also have rain or snow falling from them. On cloudy and rainy days when it seems so dark, you are probably looking at Nimbostratus clouds. Notice how parts of the clouds are darker than others. The darker parts are thicker with more water in them, so they block more of the sun's light from shining through.

Cirrus Clouds over Atkinson, NH

This type of cloud can be very pretty. They are high up in the sky where jet airplanes fly. It is so cold up there that these clouds are made out of ice crystals. The ice can form pretty shapes and patterns, and is often thin enough that these clouds don't block the whole sky, so you still see plenty of sunshine!

Contrails in Keene, NH

These clouds are "man made" by the big jet airplanes that fly very high in the sky. You've probably seen them leaving a cloud shaped like a line behind them, which is called a *contrail*. They form be-cause much of the exhaust that comes out of jet  engines is made of water. This instantly condenses into a cloud because it is so cold way up there! It can be fun to watch them after a plane moves along. Try it! Watch for a few minutes. Do they disappear because the air is so dry? Or do they stick around longer because the air has more mois-ture in it? When they last longer, sometimes they spread apart into a wider cloud. You'll find different things happen on different days, depending on how humid the air is several miles up in the sky where the jets fly. Look back at the picture of stratus clouds again (on page 12) and you'll see a contrail in the middle of the clouds that's starting to go away.

Cumulonimbus Clouds

The Thunderstorm Cloud is the "King of the clouds!" It's very tall, and it can spread out on top making it kind of look like it's wearing a "flattened hat." Since they are so high in the sky, you can see these clouds from many miles, sometimes over a hundred miles away!

Chapter 3: Precipitation Types
Snow and Sleet and Hail – Oh My!

Precipitation simply means "water that falls from the sky," that may be frozen or liquid. There are several types, and now we'll talk about why they happen and how they each form. Temperatures can change a lot from the ground up to the clouds, and this is why different kinds of precipitation fall from the sky.

Rain

Here's the easiest one: rain! When temperatures are *above* freezing (32 degrees Fahrenheit) from the clouds all the way down to the ground, then rain is what falls. Don't forget your umbrella!

Snow

Just the opposite of rain, in order for it to snow, it must be *below* the freezing temperature all the way from the clouds to the ground. So it starts as snow in the clouds and never changes all the way down. Get your sled ready!

Sleet

How is sleet made?
Mrs. Binder's 3rd graders from
Chichester Central School, Chichester, NH

Sleet is precipitation that lands on the ground as ice pellets. This happens when the temperature mid-way up in the air is above 32 degrees, but above that and down near the ground, the temperature is below freezing. So the precipitation starts out in the clouds as snow but then melts while it is falling through the air. Then as it gets near the ground and the temperatures are below freezing again, it freezes into ice.

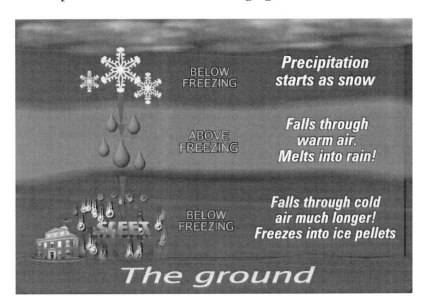

Freezing Rain

Freezing rain happens when it rains outside, but the ground is below the freezing temperature. So as soon as the raindrops hit the ground, they freeze into instant ice. Precipitation starts out as snow in the clouds but then melts on the way down. The air remains warm enough to keep the raindrops as water all the way down to the ground. Right at the ground is where the coldest air is, so everything there is below freezing and quickly turns the rainwater into ice. This

BELOW FREEZING — **Precipitation starts as snow**

ABOVE FREEZING — **Falls through warm air. Melts into rain!**

BELOW FREEZING — **Lands on cold ground — Freezes!**

ICE

The ground

can be very dangerous and causes roads, sidewalks, and driveways to be covered in a sheet of ice! This was also the reason for the big "Ice Storm" in December of 2008 that knocked down thousands of trees and caused power outages all over New England.

Route 101 in Temple, NH the day after the December, 2008 ice storm. 440,000 people in the Granite State lost their power during this storm.
Photo by Phil Reynolds

Hail

A lot of people confuse hail with sleet. That is understandable since they are both ice that falls from the sky, but they are very different. While sleet usually comes in the winter, most of the time hail falls during the warmer time of the year because it is made by thunderstorms.

Even in the summertime, far up in the sky if you go high enough, the temperature is below 32 degrees. In a thunderstorm, there are strong *updrafts*, which is air that rushes up very quickly. This happens as warm air rises, providing energy for the storm. When rain begins, if it falls into this updraft of air, it gets carried back up into the clouds again. If the updraft is strong enough, it can get carried up toward the top of the storm where the temperature is below the freezing point. When this happens, the raindrop freezes and then collides with other raindrops that are freezing too. Then this new piece of ice starts to fall again, and once again hits the updraft and gets pushed up into the freezing area

Notice how the hail is not perfectly round and there are little bumps all over it from colliding with drops of water that freeze onto it.

Look at the size of these hailstones. They're as big as baseballs! Can you imagine what it would be like if there were hundreds of baseballs coming from the sky? Hail this size can do huge damage to cars, houses and crops, and can injure people. Think about how hard they must come down from the sky when they are falling at fast speeds! When there is hail, make sure you are underneath a roof.

again, crashes into more water and ice, and keeps getting bigger!

This continues to happen until the hailstone is big and heavy enough that the updraft can no longer pick it up, so now it can keep falling to the ground. The stronger the updraft is, the bigger the hail will be because it gets carried back up into the storm more times. Since hail forms this way, it usually isn't perfectly round. If you see hail coming from a thunderstorm, you know it's probably a fairly strong one because it has updrafts big enough to make hail.

Since hail forms in layers, it's fun to cut it in half and see them! The next time a powerful thunderstorm with hail goes though your area, go outside after the storm has passed and collect many hailstones. Put them in the freezer and ask your parents to help you use a knife to cut each in half, one by one. Here's one of the biggest pieces of hail ever found, forty years ago in Kansas. See the layers inside?

CHAPTER CHALLENGES

Weather
FUN!

1) On a warm partly cloudy day, grab paper, a pencil, and an old blanket. Go outside, spread the blanket out and lie down on your back so you can see the sky. Watch the clouds drift by and notice the shapes and patterns they make. Can you picture an animal or object in the clouds? Draw what you see!

2) How many songs can you think of that have weather words in them? (Example: "Let it Snow!")

Chapter 4:

The Tools and Technology Used in Forecasting

Taking Weather Observations

A thermometer outside, showing the temperature in degrees Celsius. Zero degrees Celsius is the same as 32 degrees Fahrenheit. This is the freezing point of water. Notice how water remains frozen (in this case, as snow) under zero degrees Celsius.

Many tools are used to take weather observations; some of them you probably already have at your home or school.

You probably already know all about the thermometer! It tells you the temperature, which you can use to figure out how warm or cold it is outside. There are two ways to measure temperature in the world, Fahrenheit and Celsius. The United States uses Fahrenheit, but many other countries use Celsius. When it says 80 degrees Fahrenheit outside you can probably go out in shorts, but if it's 25 degrees you better put on a jacket! This is helpful when looking at temperatures observed all over the county or the world. Even though you aren't there, if you see a temperature of 90 in another part of the country, you know it's hot there.

Another important weather tool is an anemometer, which tells you the speed the wind is blowing. Usually it is made with three or four little tiny cups that catch wind and spin around. The faster they spin, the faster the wind! Most of the time, an anemometer is attached to a wind vane,

THE ROBINSON ANEMOMETER.

which tells you which <u>way</u> the wind is blowing. Wind direction and speed are important for two reasons: first because wind can affect you outside by making it feel colder and by blowing things around; and secondly because the direction and speed of the wind can make a big difference in the weather. For example, if the wind blows from the ocean onto land, it can cool down or warm up the weather depending on the temperature of the ocean.

The only problem with anemometers is that they are small and can't be seen from far away. Because of this, most airports also have a *windsock* so pilots can quickly find out wind speed and direction. They can easily see this instrument from a distance, as the breeze fills up the giant sock. When the

A windsock is used at most airports so pilots can quickly and easily see which way the wind is moving from far away. The wind is blowing in the direction the windsock is pointing and also in the direction of the arrows.

sock fills up with air, it points in the direction the wind is blowing. For example, with a "south wind" (wind blowing from south to north) the sock would point to the north.

If you don't have any of these things to measure the wind, try looking at the trees. When there is a gentle breeze, branches sway and leaves flip. When the wind is stronger, treetops bend and leaves may blow off.

A barometer is a very important tool to meteorologists. It measures air pressure, which can help you predict what the weather will be like. When the barometer measures higher air pressure, the weather usually gets a little bit nicer. With higher pressure, the air is heavier so it sinks and causes the clouds to evaporate away. Lower air pressure often means stormy weather is here or is getting closer. This is because lower pressure means the air is lighter, so it rises and makes clouds and showers.

A rain gauge measures how much rain falls. It is like a giant cup that collects rainwater and usually has measurements along the side. Some more expensive rain gauges actually measure it for you electronically, so you don't have to. When you know how much it has  rained by checking the rain gauge, you can keep track and find out if you're having more or less rainfall than usual. To make your own, follow the directions on page 38.

Remote Observations:
Watching the weather using technology

Many years ago, there was no way to know if bad weather was heading your way. There were no computers, telephones, or email, so you couldn't report your weather observations to someone else far away. There weren't even cars to drive and tell someone! The fastest way to get somewhere was with horse and buggy. There were certainly no satellites or radar either. Back then, you only knew a storm was coming when you saw the sky getting darker.

Today there are many ways to follow the weather all over the globe. You can check out the weather conditions practically anywhere with just the click of a computer mouse. Weather observing stations all over the world continually take readings of what the weather is like and send them out over the internet.

Rain, sleet, snow, and thunderstorms can be tracked with radar, which is a giant dish (looks like a satellite dish) that spins around in circles sending out radio waves in all directions. When a radar beam "bumps" into *precipitation*, part of the signal bounces back to the radar dish. The BIGGER the raindrop, snowflake, or hailstone is, the more of the beam that bounces back. That's how the radar knows how heavily the precipitation is coming down and where it is. Since part of the radio wave bounced back, the radar can figure out which direction and how far away the precipitation is.

There are hundreds of radar dishes in the United States that can sense precipitation within about 140 miles or so. To

This is the radar station that watches over much of New Hampshire and Maine. It is located in Gray, Maine and operated by the National Weather Service. The radar dish that spins around is inside that giant dome (the big ball) at the top. The dome keeps the spinning dish from getting snow or rain on it.

Photo by John Jensenius

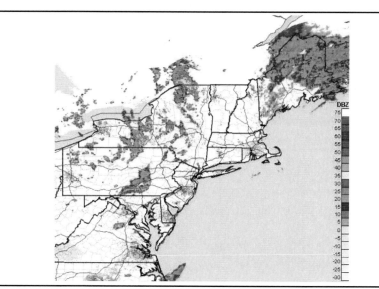

A radar picture can show you where there is rain, snow, or sleet. Which New England state is getting a lot of rain right now in this radar picture?

This is one of the satellites that fly miles above the Earth, taking pictures of the clouds and beaming them back.

drive this far in your car would take around three hours. All the radar dishes together cover the entire country, plus just over 100 miles out over the ocean.

Clouds can be watched from satellites out in space. Each one rotates with the Earth's spin, so it's always hovering right over the same spot. All the satellites keep taking pictures of the clouds so that we can see where they go, as well as what types of clouds they are. They also take pictures of hurricanes out in the middle of the ocean, so we know where they are and where they are heading. Since radar signals can't reach into the middle of the ocean, satellites are the most important way of tracking hurricanes.

The National Weather Service launches weather balloons all over the country two times every day. They travel way up into the air and carry weather tools that measure conditions high in the sky.

Photo by John Jensenius

Since they are bigger than normal balloons, they can travel much higher into the sky.

Photo by John Jensenius

Before computers were invented, forecasting the weather was not very accurate. The reason is that in order to predict the weather more than a few hours ahead, we needed to do billions of math problems - that's something impossible for human beings to do in a short time! (Besides, would you really want to do billions of math problems?)

It would take humans thousands of years to do the calculations that the computers do in a couple of hours. So you see why we *need* computers to help us.

Here is one of the supercomputers that calculates weather predictions and helps meteorologists make their forecast. Those stacks of computer equipment are all part of the *same* computer, which takes up a whole room! This is one of the most powerful computers in the world.

Every day, around 100 million weather observations are put into these supercomputers. These are weather conditions from around the world, includ-

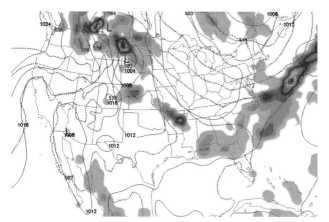

This computer model map shows areas in the United States that might have rain or snow soon.

ing weather information at airports, from ships at sea, from airplanes, weather balloons, and more. Then the computer takes all these weather numbers and calculates what the weather will do in the future. The computer forecasts are not always right, so meteorologists look at them and use their experience and education to decide if they are correct.

Sometimes the computers can be wrong because not enough weather data was used, and sometimes because weather is so complicated that it can't always be figured out just by doing math problems. Most of the time the computer forecasts are very close and when a meteorologist looks at maps from the computer, he or she can get a good idea of what the weather will be in the future.

CHAPTER CHALLENGES

1) To measure wind speed, follow these directions to make your own simple outdoor anemometer:

Equipment:

1. 3 straws that are at least eight inches long
2. 4 plastic 3-ounce cups
3. 2-liter plastic bottle that has been filled with sand
4. 18 to 24-inch wooden dowel that will fit into the bottle opening AND into the straw opening
5. push pin
6. pencil with a NEW eraser
7. stapler

Directions:

A) Find the center of 2 of the straws and put marks there.

B) Pull or cut off the small eraser on the pencil. Carefully push it into the opening of the 3rd straw.

C) Staple a cup under-neath the end of each straw "arm." Be sure the 2 cups on each straw arm are facing the opposite direction.

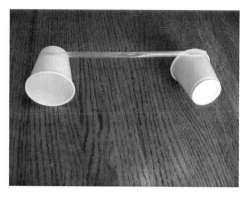

D) Cross the 2 straws that have the cups at the center points you marked so they are in an "X" shape.

E) Push the push pin through both straws at the center and into the pencil eraser.

F) Slide the "up and down" straw onto the long wooden dowel.

G) Push dowel into the sand in the 2 liter container.

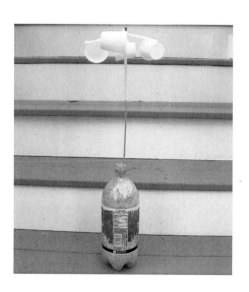

H) Place your anemom-eter in an open area and not near a building.

2) Make a rain gauge! Use a clear plastic container such as an empty peanut butter jar to measure rain fall. Either tape a plastic ruler inside the jar or use a permanent marker to write measurements on the outside of the jar. Place the container in an outside place in an open place away from dripping roofs.

3) Use the link: www.n2yo.com to find out exactly where weather satellites are above the earth right now. This site always shows where the International Space Station is on a map. You can click on other satellite names at the top of the page, such as "GOES 10." You can also click on "NOAA" to find other weather satellites.

4) The link radar.weather.gov/index.htm can be used to look at the weather radar all over the United States.

If you have trouble finding any of the websites in this book, simply go to www.weatherfactsandfun.com for a list.

Chapter 5:

Weather Maps and Symbols

As you've seen so far, there are many different types of weather observations. There are temperature observations, wind speed and direction measurements, and of course we have to know what the sky is doing in the area we're watching! Is it sunny,

"Full Blown Cloud"
By Alex Mitchell and
Seamus Dolan
Grade 5
Teacher: Ms. Cummings
Hampstead Middle School

cloudy, raining, or snowing? Is there a thundershower, or any other type of storminess? You'll remember that these are important things for weather forecasters to know. So how do they take all this information and make it easy to understand quickly? One way is to put it all on a map, using weather symbols.

Meteorologists make maps with weather symbols so that they can look at them quickly to know the weather all around their area. There are symbols that show what is happening in the sky, what the wind is doing, and what the temperature is. It makes it easy for weather forecasters to quickly learn what it's like all around, and if bad weather might be coming toward them.

Now let's learn how to make weather symbols for each place that has a weather observation. This is called a "station plot." The majority of these are from weather observations taken at airports.

Step 1: We start off with a circle. Inside the circle, we will show how many clouds are in the sky. If it is sunny with almost no clouds, we leave the circle empty.

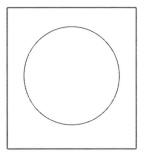

The more clouds in the sky, the more we color in the circle; if clouds cover about half the sky then color the circle in halfway. When it is completely cloudy, we color the circle all the way in like the second plot.

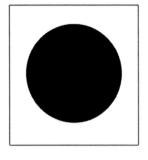

Now, with a very quick look, we can tell how cloudy or sunny the sky is!

Step 2: Next, we'll do the temperature. We put it just to the left and up a bit from our sunny weather symbol. Let's say the temperature is 75 degrees Fahrenheit, so we put that next to the circle like this:

Now we know it's sunny and 75 degrees! OK, let's try some more.

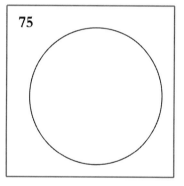

Step 3: We need to show both the wind speed and the DIRECTION. Wind gets named from the direction on a compass that it comes from. So a wind that is blowing from north to south is called a "north wind." A wind that comes from the west and blows toward the east is called a "west wind." If a wind is blowing from the southwest, what is it called?

Now on our station plot, we draw a line showing the direction of the wind.

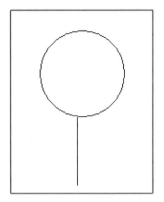

A "south wind" which blows from the bottom of the map to the top (south to north) would be a line that goes in that direction and connects to our weather symbol like the top picture.

Here's how we draw a "northwest wind" which shows the wind blowing from the northwest:

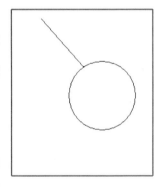

This picture helps you tell which way the wind is coming from, and what to name it. The arrows point in the direction the wind is blowing. Use this to help you figure out which way to draw the lines on your station plot.

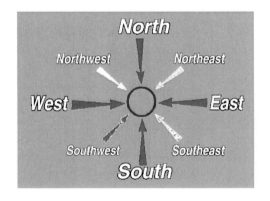

Step 4: Now it's time to add the wind SPEED! At the end of the line, you draw another line to show how fast the wind is blowing. A short line means about 5 miles per hour, a long line is about 10 miles per hour. (Meteorologists sometimes measure the wind in *knots*, which is another way to measure speed, but we'll use miles per hour in this book.)

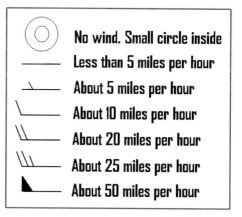

(circle symbol)	No wind. Small circle inside
——	Less than 5 miles per hour
(symbol)	About 5 miles per hour
(symbol)	About 10 miles per hour
(symbol)	About 20 miles per hour
(symbol)	About 25 miles per hour
(symbol)	About 50 miles per hour

A small circle inside means there is no wind at all. When you just draw a line, the winds are less than 5 miles per hour (mph). One short little line means around 5 mph, and a longer line means somewhere about 10 mph. The flag at the bottom means about 50 mph!

Here's a station plot for a day that is 75 degrees, sunny, with winds coming from the southwest at around 15 miles per hour. Sounds like a nice day!

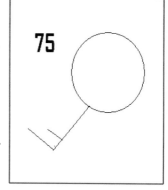

Step 5: Finally, there's one last detail to add to our weather observation! We have shown the clouds, winds, and temperature. Now we report if there are any other weather conditions, such as snow, rain, fog, or anything else we should tell people about.

Here is a chart with a lot of "present weather" symbols on it. We take one of these and put it under the temperature on our weather observation.

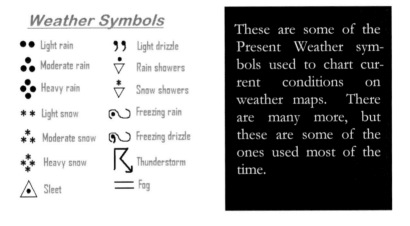

Weather Symbols

●● Light rain   🎵 Light drizzle

●● Moderate rain   ▽ Rain showers

●●● Heavy rain   ▽ Snow showers

✱ ✱ Light snow   ∿ Freezing rain

✱ ✱ Moderate snow   ∿ Freezing drizzle

✱✱✱ Heavy snow   R Thunderstorm

△ Sleet   ═ Fog

These are some of the Present Weather symbols used to chart current conditions on weather maps. There are many more, but these are some of the ones used most of the time.

So now let's say it's lightly snowing. We take the two small snowflakes and put them to the left of our weather observation plot. Let's make a day that has cloudy skies, is 25 degrees, with the winds blowing at 25 mph from the northeast, and it is lightly snowing. That would be a snowy, windy, and cold day for sure! Here's what our station plot looks like:

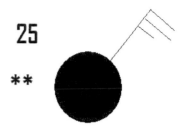

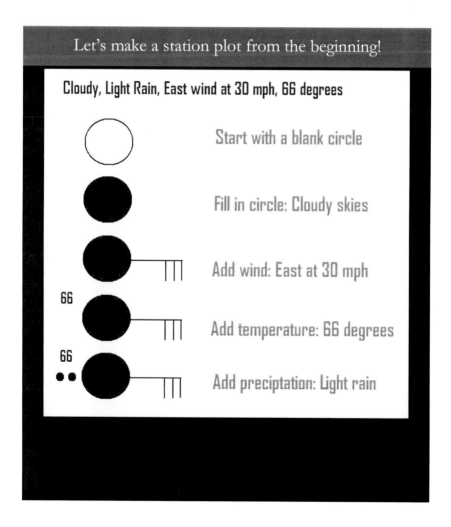

Let's make a station plot from the beginning!

Cloudy, Light Rain, East wind at 30 mph, 66 degrees

Start with a blank circle

Fill in circle: Cloudy skies

Add wind: East at 30 mph

Add temperature: 66 degrees

Add preciptation: Light rain

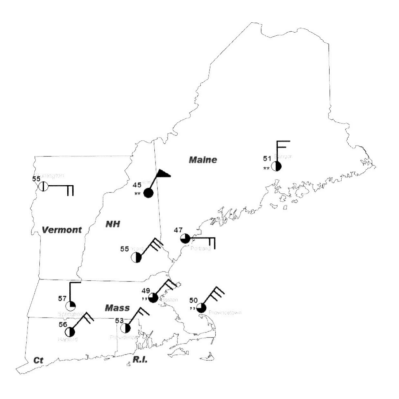

Notice anything interesting about the weather on this particular day? Winds are coming from over the ocean either from the northeast or the east in most places. Did you notice that it's cloudier and cooler in areas closer to the ocean? It is also raining or there is light drizzle closer to the sea as well. Look how it's sunnier and warmer in cities farther away from the Atlantic Ocean, in western parts of New England. It's also very windy in northern NH in the mountains!

Now that you know how to read and draw weather observation plots, use the pull-out map in this book to plot your own weather! There are several sets of weather conditions for you to try, or use real weather observations! Find out where to get the real weather conditions at this book's website: www.weatherfactsandfun.com

Why do we want to know where the wind is coming from?

Wind direction and speed are very important to meteorologists, because wind can change the weather and what it feels like. On a windy day, being outside might not be as fun as other days. Wind also blows things around and can make it feel colder than it really is outside.

The direction that the wind comes from can be very important, too. Wind can bring warm or cold air to you, so if the wind comes from a place that is very cold, it can make the temperature much colder. In New England, wind often comes from the ocean. When this happens it can make it feel

When wind starts over the ocean and moves onto land, it can change the weather and sometimes bring rain. In the summer, the cool ocean water makes the air above it chilly – so when the chilly wind moves over land, it cools all of us down. In the winter, sometimes the ocean water is warmer than the air and can actually warm us up a little bit. It can even change snow into rain!

When you think of down south, what do you think about? Maybe warm weather in places like Florida? Well, when the wind comes from the south, or especially the southwest, it brings that warmer air up to us! On days when there is a southwest wind, New England usually has much warmer weather.

very cold and sometimes brings rain, drizzle, or even snow from the water in the sea!

CHAPTER CHALLENGES

1) Go to **vortex.plymouth.edu** on the internet and find out what the weather is like right now in Phoenix, Arizona; Minneapolis, Minnesota; and Miami, Florida. How is the weather in these places different from yours?

2) Write weather words such as RAIN, SNOW, WIND, FOG, SUNNY on separate index cards. How would you act out each of these words without talking?

WEATHER OBSERVATIONS

Name_____

Directions: On this chart, write down weather data every day at the same time for a week (longer if you want!) Look at the movement of tree leaves and branches to see if it's windy.

Date/Time	Temperature	Is it Windy?	Weather Conditions (Cloudy? Rainy? Sunny?)

After a week, look at your data. How did the measurements change each day? You can try this same activity in a different season and compare the results.

This page is free to copy for educational purposes. From www.weatherfactsandfun.com

Chapter 6:

Stormy Weather

One of the biggest reasons we have weather on Earth is because of our sun. The sun heats the Earth to keep us warm, but it doesn't do it evenly. Some areas get more sun and warmth than others (because the Earth is not flat), and weather is caused when the warm and cold air tries to become equal.

Just think about it. When you open a window in the winter, the cold air comes right in the window. That is the cold air trying to even out the temperature because it's much warmer inside. This same thing happens all over the Earth as warm and cold air are constantly rushing around the planet trying to "even out" the planet to one temperature. This will never happen, but that doesn't mean the air won't keep on trying. In fact, the more it tries, the more types of weather it creates!

You've seen how hot air balloons rise. Warm air always rises because it weighs less than cold air. So when the sun warms us up on a hot day, the warm air it creates goes up high into the sky. When this warm air lifts, it cools off and creates clouds high up in the air. Since the air cools off up there, it can't hold the water vapor anymore and so the water turns into clouds. Sometimes this even causes rain or snow! If it's really hot, and the conditions are right, there can even be storms.

> **When the sky is red or pink at night, is it true that means that the next day is going to be hot? If so, why?**
> Michaela Murphy-Woo, Derry, NH

There is an old saying that is also close to this that goes like this: "*Red sky at night, sailor's delight. Red sky in the morning, sailors take warning.*" Sailors used this a long time ago to help them know what weather to expect the next day.

Why would a red sky at night make a sailor so happy? Well, our sky usually turns red or pink during sunset and sunrise if there is nice weather. Since most of the time our weather comes to us from the west, if you look in the sky in that direction you can often see the weather heading this way. The sun also sets in the west... Soooo... this means that if the sky is red at sunset, then the weather is nice to our west and good weather must be coming this way! (This isn't always true, but a lot of the time it works.)

OK, so why would a sailor have to take warning if the sky was red in the morning? Since the sun *RISES* in the east, then good weather in the east might mean that the nice weather is going away!

There are many types of storms. Let's take a look at some of the ones you may know best.

THUNDERSTORMS

A thunderstorm is any storm that has thunder and lightning. These can form when warm or hot air rises quickly into the atmosphere. If it is humid out, this can help the air lift even faster! It goes up and turns into clouds and rain. Then it continues climbing, which makes even more clouds and rain. Pretty soon it's a really tall cloud with lots of rain in it, and lightning and thunder begin.

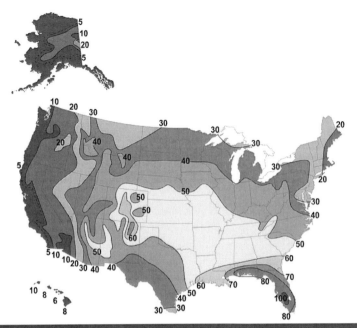

This map shows the average number of thunderstorms in a year around the United States. Can you find the parts of the country that get the smallest number of storms? Check out Florida for the most!

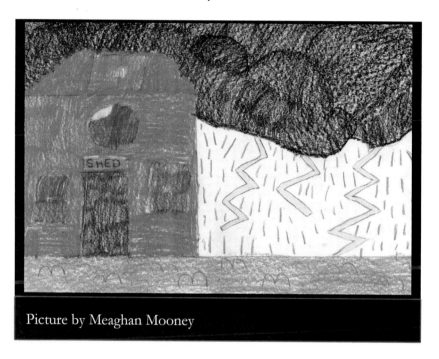

Picture by Meaghan Mooney

Thunderstorms often pop up where warm and cool air meet. Remember how we said not everywhere gets heated up the same amount by the sun? This area is sort of a "battle zone" where the warm and cold air bump into each other trying to "even out"… just like the cold air that tries to rush into your bedroom window. This "battle" creates rising air and forms rain, sleet, or snow… and very often thunderstorms. The hotter the air, the stronger the storm may be.

Here in New England, most places see somewhere around twenty days with thunderstorms every year. Some years there are a little more than that and some years a little less. Parts of the country farther to our south get many more than that. Florida is the state with the most thunderstorms where some areas see them up to 100 days a year. Wow!

The most dangerous part of a thunderstorm is lightning. Lightning is a form of static electricity. Have you ever dragged your feet across the floor and then touched somebody and felt a static shock? That's the same kind of electricity that lightning is. Lightning can be as hot as 50 THOUSAND degrees Fahrenheit! Since it is made of electricity, it is important to stay in a safe place when a thunderstorm is near you.

How does thunder make a sound?
E. Katerina Sekella, Greenfield Elementary School

You can't have thunder without lightning, because thunder is the SOUND of lightning! Because lightning is so hot, as it travels through the sky, the air quickly moves away from the hot electricity - very quickly! It moves SO fast that it makes a sound as it rips across the sky, and that is the sound of thunder. So the next time you hear thunder, you will know that it is actually the air saying "Ouch!!!"

Weather
FACT

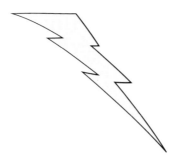

Some people say that lightning never strikes the same place twice. This is not true, especially for tall and pointy objects. The Empire State Building in New York City gets hit about 25 times a year!

Lightning from a thunderstorm in the Lakes Region of New Hampshire.

Where do you think is the safest place to be when a thunderstorm is nearby?

a) In your car?

b) Playing on a swing set?

c) In your house?

d) Climbing a tree?

Weather FACT

What did you answer? Well, lightning is attracted to tall things, so climbing a tree certainly wouldn't be a very good idea! And a swing set also would be pretty dangerous, especially a metal one. The correct answer is in your

When you see lightning and hear thunder, you can tell about how far away the storm is. After you see the lightning, count how many seconds it takes to hear the thunder.

For every five seconds, the storm is one mile away. So if you count slowly to ten the storm is two miles away.

Many of our stronger thunderstorms produce hail that can fall at speeds up to 100 miles per hour. As you know, hail forms in layers when it is carried up and down inside the storm. This is a picture of the largest piece of hail ever found in the United States. It was 18.75 inches around and fell in Aurora, Nebraska on June 22, 2003. You can clearly see that hail isn't always round.

house, because that provides the best protection. The second best place to be if there isn't a building nearby, is in a vehicle. Cars are not safer because of the rubber tires, but because of something called the "skin effect," which means that the lightning hits the car and just travels through the "skin," which is the outside part of the car.

Thunderstorms may have heavy rain and gusty winds that can do damage to houses or trees. On a day when thunderstorms might happen, a "Thunderstorm Watch" is issued by forecasters. This doesn't mean a storm will form, but is a way for you to know to pay attention to the sky. When a thunderstorm is headed your way, a "Thunderstorm Warning" is declared. This means you should go indoors right away and wait for the storm to pass so that you stay safe.

A very strong type of wind gust that can come from thunderstorms is called a *microburst*. This is caused when very cold air builds up in a thundercloud and then suddenly breaks loose and falls toward the ground. When it hits the ground it spreads out in all directions and causes wind up to 100 miles per hour or more! That's a lot faster than your parents drive on the highway. (Or if they do they'll get a very big ticket!) Microburst winds knock down trees and buildings, and sometimes they are so strong that people think a tornado was there.

A microburst knocked down trees in a forest. Notice how they are all facing the same direction from the strong wind that tipped them over.

This NASA picture shows what a microburst would be like at an airport. Airplane pilots don't take off and land under thunderstorms, just in case a microburst happens. Look at how the wind drops down from the clouds and then goes out in all directions at a very high speed.

TORNADOES AND WATERSPOUTS

You've probably heard a lot of things about tornadoes. They are very strong and dangerous and come from severe thunderstorms. A tornado is a violent wind that swirls around in circles very fast. It is connected from the cloud right to the ground. If it is not touching the ground then it's called a funnel cloud and is not a tornado. Some "twisters" are only strong enough to knock down small trees, but some are much more powerful and can destroy a house in seconds.

Anywhere on Earth could have a tornado, but there are some areas where they happen a lot more than other places. New England doesn't have very many of them, but there are usually a couple every year. The chances of you seeing a tornado are *very* low. Most people have never seen one because they don't happen very often and because they aren't big enough to cover a lot of area. If there was a tornado on the other side of your town, you might not even know it. So while being prepared for a tornado is a very good idea, you probably will never see one in your life, except on TV or in pictures.

The winds in a tornado can be up to 200 miles per hour or even higher. That's faster than some racecars! The biggest danger to people from a tornado is that it picks things up and blows them all around, and you can get hit by these flying objects. If you ever were to see one come to your house (this will probably never happen) the best place to go is down into your basement. You might want to talk to your parents about this and come up with a plan of where you would go to be safe.

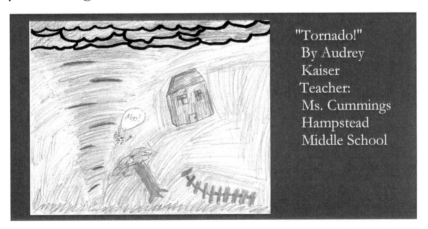

"Tornado!"
By Audrey Kaiser
Teacher: Ms. Cummings
Hampstead Middle School

Why do most tornadoes form in Tornado Alley?
Andrew B., Hampstead Middle School, Hampstead, NH

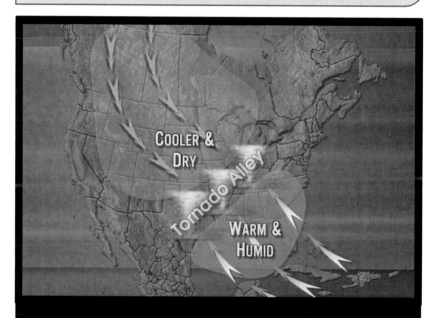

Warm and humid air rushes up from the south and cool and drier air comes down from the north. When they collide, it can sometimes help form a tornado.

Tornadoes happen the most in the middle of our country, in an area most people call "Tornado Alley" because there are many more of them there than in other places.

Weather FACT

Even though we don't live in Tornado Alley, we still do have tornadoes here in New England most years. Look at the map and see the *average* number of tornadoes. Average means that most years we have this many but not every year; some years a little more and some years a little less.

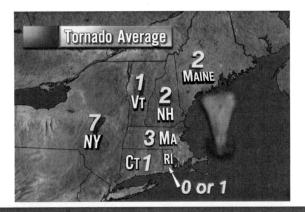

Here is the average number of tornadoes each year for the states around where we live. Is this more or less than you thought? Most tornadoes around New England are very small and weak, but can still do some damage.

A waterspout is a tornado that is over water. When a tornado travels over water, it sucks water up inside and it spins around very quickly. From far away, they can actually look quite pretty, but they are very dangerous to boaters. Waterspouts are usually not as strong as tornadoes on land.

A water spout is a tornado that is over water.

7/25/2008 2:16:13 PM (-4.0 hrs) Lat=43.21574 Lon=-71.27111 Alt=1565ft MSL WGS 84

One of the strongest tornadoes in recent New England history struck eleven towns in New Hampshire in July 2008. Here is a look at some of the damage in Deerfield, NH, where several houses were completely destroyed. The tornado had winds up to 120 miles per hour.

One thing we all have to do after a snowstorm is shovel the snow away!

Weather
FUN!

Have you ever had "Sugar and Snow?"
After it snows, go outside and scoop up some snow in a bowl. Make sure it is clean snow from a snowstorm that just happened, and that nobody has walked on it yet. Then, come inside and pour maple syrup on the snow and eat it up! It is very yummy!

SNOWSTORMS AND BLIZZARDS

Different people like different kinds of weather. Some people love snowstorms and some people hate them. A lot of kids enjoy storms because they are able to go outside and play in the snow! Many parents probably don't like them quite as much because they have to drive on slippery roads and shovel the snow, and many parts of life get a little harder. One thing everyone agrees on is that when winter storms come, everyone notices.

Shoveling out from a big snowstorm can take a long time, especially when your car is covered like this! Looks like somebody isn't going to be happy about having to clean off this car!

Snowstorms can have very heavy snow that piles up into huge snow banks, or they can be light with only enough snow to just cover the ground. It all depends on how much water is in the storm clouds. Some of the biggest storms in New England have brought more than three FEET of snow! The number of snowstorms and amount of snow that we get changes every year. There have been some years when the ground had no snow for a lot of the winter and some where it took until the middle of spring for it all to melt.

Years that have a lot of snow can also cause problems when it melts in the spring. When a lot of it melts all at once, the rivers and streams fill up with water and sometimes they can't hold it all. That can lead to flooding.

What is the difference between a blizzard and a snow-storm?
Andrew Buczynski, home school, Hudson, NH

A blizzard is a snowstorm with strong winds that blows the snow around so much that you can't see very well.

Traveling in a car or truck can be difficult when you can't see very far ahead of you, so driving in blizzards is dangerous.

In order to be officially called a blizzard, a snowstorm has to have winds of 35 miles per hour or higher, and you can't see more than ¼ of a mile. These two things have to happen for at least three hours for the storm to be called a blizzard.

Did you know a storm can even be a blizzard when it's not snowing? As long as the wind is strong enough and you can't see farther than a ¼ mile because of the blowing snow, it's a blizzard!

NOR'EASTERS

Here in New England, we get a lot of storms called "Nor'easters." Most people don't know exactly what this means except that we can get a lot of snow. Well, after reading this, you'll be able to teach your parents about what a Nor'easter is. Won't they be impressed!

Nor'easters often have heavy snow that falls quickly and piles up high! Some years we have many of them and some only a few. The thing that makes a storm a Nor'easter is the direction the winds blow from. Remember back in chapter 5 when you learned that winds get their name from the direction they blow *from*? Winds from a Nor'easter come from – yup, you guessed it - the northeast! This doesn't

This is what a Nor'easter looks like on radar.

Notice that there is precipitation in New England and beyond.

always happen during the whole storm because the winds change direction as the storm passes by. Since the wind usually comes from the ocean toward the land, there can sometimes be flooding at the coast as well. This happens when ocean water gets blown onto land.

Believe it or not, Nor'easters aren't only winter storms. They happen just as often in the fall and spring. Since it's warmer then, we get lots rain instead of snow.

This type of storm was named back in colonial times hundreds of years ago, when we had no satellites or radar. People didn't know where the storm was coming from, but they did know that the winds were blowing from the north-east, so that's what they named it. The funny thing is that

Nor'easters don't usually come from the northeast, they usually come from the south or southwest - but they didn't know that back then.

HURRICANES

Hurricanes are very large, monster storms. They can cause a lot of damage, and since they're so big, they often cover many states at once. While their winds aren't quite as strong as some tornadoes, they are thousands of times bigger and affect many more people.

Hurricane season begins every year on June 1st and lasts until November 30th. That's six months long! Most of these storms hap- pen when it's hurricane sea- son, but some- times they do form before or afterwards. They usually

start during the summer and fall because that's when the ocean is the warmest, and warm ocean water is needed for a hurricane to form. In fact, the ocean water needs to be at least 80 degrees Fahrenheit for one to occur. They also usually begin their journey down near the Earth's equator, where the water is the warmest, and then they sometimes travel north towards the United States and other countries.

There has never been a hurricane season without a hurricane. The smallest number ever for a season in the Atlantic Ocean was two storms. Sometimes there can be many at one time; the most ever at the same time was four. Usually if two big storms come near each other they will "bounce off" each other or "dance" around one other. There have even been a few times when a bigger hurricane "ate up" a smaller one and they combined into one! The last time this happened was in 1995 when Hurricane Humberto absorbed Iris.

Some hurricanes move from the water onto land, and sometimes they just stay out at sea. When they do run into land, they start to slowly get weaker because there is no more warm water to give them energy.

A group of very brave airplane pilots and meteorologists called *Hurricane Hunters* actually fly their planes IN-

Here's one of the airplanes that *Hurricane Hunters* use to fly into these storms. They are built extra strong to stand up to the dangerous winds.

SIDE hurricanes to find out how strong they are! Can you imagine flying through a storm like that? After they get inside, the airplane drops instruments into the storm to measure wind speed and direction, temperatures, and many other important things to help figure out where the hurricane will go and how much damage it could do.

A satellite picture of Hurricane Katrina in August 2005, which did major damage to the city of New Orleans in the southern part of the United States. Thousands of homes were destroyed and the city was evacuated. It is still slowly being rebuilt today.

> **Is it possible to have a thunderstorm, a hurricane and a tornado at the same time?**
> Sarah, Henry W. Moore School, Candia, NH

A hurricane can do damage in many ways. The winds can be very strong and blow down houses and trees. They also push a lot of water onto land which is called "Storm Surge." When this happens, entire cities and towns can be flooded. Thunderstorms and tornadoes also usually arrive with hurricanes, so we can have all three at one time. Yikes!

> **Why do hurricanes have names?**
> Zachary Thornton, Greenfield Elementary School

Hurricanes are named so that we can tell them apart. Imagine if there were two or three of them out in the ocean at once. How would you know which was which? Before 1950, hurricanes were not named, and it was confusing! At first, they were given just female names, and then in 1979 meteorologists started using male names, too.

There are six lists of names and once they get to the end of the list, they go back to the beginning again. So some names are used over and over. If a hurricane is really bad, they will stop using the name and pick a new one to use in

Hurricane Names

2010

Alex	Fiona	Karl	Paula
Bonnie	Gaston	Lisa	Richard
Colin	Hermine	Matthew	Shary
Danielle	Igor	Nicole	Tomas
Earl	Julia	Otto	Virginie
			Walter

2011

Arlene	Franklin	Katia	Philippe
Bret	Gert	Lee	Rina
Cindy	Harvey	Maria	Sean
Don	Irene	Nate	Tammy
Emily	Jose	Ophelia	Vince
			Whitney

2012

Alberto	Florence	Kirk	Patty
Beryl	Gordon	Leslie	Rafael
Chris	Helene	Michael	Sandy
Debby	Isaac	Nadine	Tony
Ernesto	Joyce	Oscar	Valerie
			William

2013

Andrea	Fernand	Karen	Pablo
Barry	Gabrielle	Lorenzo	Rebekah
Chantal	Humberto	Melissa	Sebastien
Dorian	Ingrid	Nestor	Tanya
Erin	Jerry	Olga	Van
			Wendy

2014

Arthur	Fay	Kyle	Paulette
Bertha	Gonzalo	Laura	Rene
Cristobal	Hanna	Marco	Sally
Dolly	Isaias	Nana	Teddy
Edouard	Josephine	Omar	Vicky
			Wilfred

Storms are named by the World Meteorology Organization. There are people from many countries in this group. They meet each year to decide if any hurricanes were bad enough to stop using that name. They add new names when needed.

its place. Check out the list on the previous page. Is your name on it? If it isn't, then it might never be a hurricane name *unless* there's a bad storm and they replace one of these names with yours. Or it could have been a dangerous storm already so the name isn't used anymore.

Hurricanes usually start as a bunch of thunderstorms or showers (this is called a "tropical wave") but when they travel over the warm ocean, and the conditions in our atmosphere are right, they start to grow.

As the winds get stronger, a *tropical depression* forms. This is when the winds are less than 38 miles per hour. If it continues to get stronger, it turns into a *Tropical Storm,* with winds between 39-73 miles per hour. Once it becomes a tropical storm, it gets a name. If the winds reach 74 mph or higher, it is officially a hurricane!

There are five categories of hurricanes. This is called the "Saffir-Simpson Scale."

Category 1: Winds from 74-95 miles per hour

Small damage to buildings, branches will snap off trees and

some small trees and telephone poles could be knocked down, causing power to go out in some spots.

Category 2: Winds from 96-110 miles per hour

House siding and parts of the windows and shingles on the roof may blow off. Older mobile homes can suffer quite a bit of damage. Some poorly built signs will be blown down. Many trees and telephone poles will be knocked down causing widespread power outages.

Category 3: Winds from 111-130 miles per hour

Many homes will be damaged. Some windows will be blown out of high rise buildings. Many poorly built signs will be blown down. Lots of trees and telephone poles will be knocked down and almost all houses in the area will lose electricity for days or weeks.

Category 4: Winds from 131-155 miles per hour

The walls and roofs of a lot of homes are destroyed, with complete destruction to older mobile homes. Most signs are blown down. Many windows will be blown out of high rise buildings. Hundreds or thousands of fallen trees and telephone poles will block roads and leave most areas with no electricity for weeks.

Category 5: Winds are above 155 miles per hour

Many houses and business are completely destroyed, blown over, or even blown away! Complete destruction to all mobile homes. All signs are blown down. Nearly all windows are blown out of high rise buildings. Most of the trees

The wind in a hurricane travels in a circle around the "eye," which has no clouds or wind at all! When the eye goes overhead, you can usually see blue sky and some people think the hurricane is gone, only to have the bad weather return when the other side moves in.

and telephone poles will be knocked down and will block areas off and cause electricity to be lost for weeks or months.

Obviously, the stronger the winds, the more damage a hurricane can do! That's why we keep track of what category it is, so that we know how much we need to prepare and how much damage to expect. Hurricanes can form in many parts

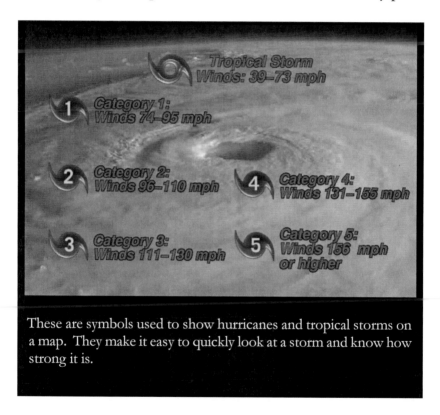

These are symbols used to show hurricanes and tropical storms on a map. They make it easy to quickly look at a storm and know how strong it is.

of the world, but not all countries call them hurricanes. They are called *tropical cyclones* in some places, and on the other side of the world near China and Japan, they are *typhoons*. They are all the same type of storm, just with different names.

Storms and the highest New England winds

Here in New England, hurricanes aren't as common as in some other parts of the country because they have to travel farther north to get here, and move over colder water. They do sometimes hit us, but their winds are not always at full hurricane force anymore because the storm has weakened. Recent storms to affect us here, after they lost some of their wind speed, are listed on the next two pages:

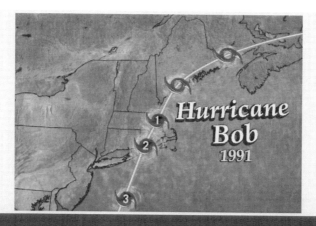

Hurricane Bob – August 1991:
Winds between 70-100 mph
Bob did the worst damage to southern parts of New England and areas near the New Hampshire seacoast region. Many houses lost electricity for several days or up to a week. The numbers on the hurricane in the picture show the strength of the storm.

Hurricane Floyd – September 1999:
Winds between 50-60 mph (a tropical storm when it reached us)
Floyd came up at us almost the same way as Bob did, but was not quite as strong. Just like Bob, the worst wind damage was in southern New England and near the New Hampshire seacoast region. Flooding happened in Belknap, Cheshire, and Grafton Counties of New Hampshire.

Hurricane Gloria – September 1985:
Winds between 65-85 mph
Gloria also came up from our south, but was farther west. Almost every part of New England saw some storminess. Many people put tape on their windows, thinking that it would stop them from shattering.

Weather
FACT

According to the National Hurricane Center, putting tape on your windows before a hurricane arrives is a waste of time, effort, and tape! It does not stop windows from shattering or stop pieces of glass from flying across a room. You should either stay far away from windows, or put wooden boards over the windows instead.

As tropical storms and hurricanes move through the ocean and over land, it can be fun to track them. You can use the hurricane tracking chart in this book to see where they come from and where they go, and how strong they are. You can get information on how to track them at: www.weatherfactsandfun.com.

Weather
FACT

Most grownups can usually lean into a 70 mile per hour wind and not fall over.

Most people can NOT walk into a 90 mile per hour wind without holding on to something like a railing.

A 130 mile per hour wind can lift most grownups off the ground!

Hurricanes don't have the strongest winds on Earth! The highest wind gust ever recorded in the world was at the top of Mount Washington in New Hampshire. On April 10, 1934 a wind gust of 231 miles per hour was measured.

CHAPTER CHALLENGES

1) If a thunderstorm is not very close by, you see the lightning before you hear the thunder. This is because light travels faster than sound. What are other examples of seeing an action and then

hearing the sound a bit later? (To get you started: One example would be seeing fireworks and not hearing the boom right away.)

2) Look at the map on the next page that shows the average tornadoes in the United States in one year. Which states do you think are in "Tornado Alley" and why?

3) Go to the site: www.intellicast.com/Storm/Severe/Lightning.aspx to see where lightning strikes are happening in the United States right now!

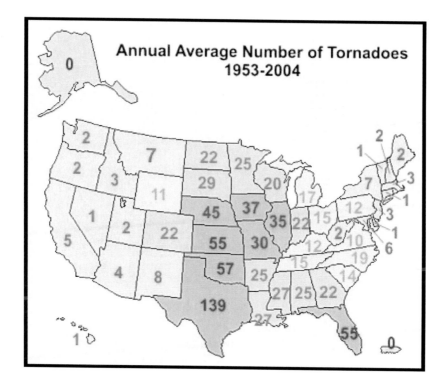

Annual Average Number of Tornadoes 1953-2004

4) Snowflake collecting activity: This activity keeps snowflakes forever without a freezer!

Equipment: clear plastic spray such as Krylon™; plastic page protectors that are "crinkly" and don't feel like vinyl. Be sure all the equipment is COLD before you begin.

A) Check to see that the falling snowflakes are perfect flakes and not ice crystals or pieces of flakes.

B) Spray the cold page protector with the cold clear plastic spray.

C) Let snowflakes fall into the spray so a single layer is formed. Do not let flakes fall on top of each other.

D) Put the page protector in a protected place OUTSIDE so it can dry and no more flakes can fall on it.

E) Once it has completely dried, it can be brought inside and looked at with a magnifying glass or a 30X microviewer.

WHY THIS WORKS: As the snowflake evaporates, it leaves its "print" in the plastic.

TRACKING A HURRICANE

Use the hurricane tracking map that came with this book. Ask an adult for help getting started.

If you're reading this book between June 1st and November 30th, go to **nhc.noaa.gov** to see if there are any tropical storms or hurricanes in the Atlantic Ocean. If there are no storms in the Atlantic right now, use the coordinates from Hurricane Floyd listed below.

Date	Latitude	Longitude	Wind Speed	Category
9/10	19	59	80	1
9/11	22	62	110	2
9/12	23	66	120	3
9/13	24	71	155	4
9/14	25	76	120	3
9/15	29	79	115	3
9/16	36	77	80	1
9/17	43	71	50	Tropical Storm
9/18	47	63	40	Strong Storm

Helpful Hints: Latitude is the line that goes back and forth from one side to the other, and longitude goes up and down. Once you find the numbers on the sides and bottom, find where they meet to see the location of the storm. Locations are listed by the date the observations were taken, so put a dot where the storm was each day. Next to the dot, write the date and wind speed, or hurricane category if you wish.

Chapter 7:

Fun Weather!

(Fun, strange or sometimes crazy things to see)

Rainbow

You probably know what rainbows are! They form when there is rain falling but also some sun is shining through the rain. Light looks white but is actually filled with colors that you don't see. As the sun shines through the water, the light gets bent in a way that lets the colors out. This usually happens late in the day when the sun is lower in the sky and can shine under the rainclouds.

Challenge! On a sunny day, go outside to your garden hose that has a sprayer on the end. Spray the water up into the air and look at the water. If the sun is shining brightly enough you will see a rainbow in the water.

Rainbow around the sun

Remember those Cirrus clouds that are way high up in the sky and made of ice? Well, sometimes if the sun is shining through them, the clouds bend some of the sunlight just right to form a rainbow that makes a circle around the sun. When this happens, it's best to use sunglasses and try not to look directly at the sun so you don't hurt your eyes.

Photo courtesy: www.borealisimages.ca

Sun Pillars

They're quite beautiful, aren't they? They are a shaft of sunlight that goes up and down. Sun pillars form when light from the rising or setting sun reflects off ice crystals in the air.

Sun Dogs

Sun Dogs appear for the same reason as sun pillars. Sunlight reflects off ice crystals in the air making it look like there are THREE suns! The big one in the middle is the real sun, and two smaller suns on each side are the reflections. Have you ever seen sun dogs? They don't happen very often. Did you also notice that there is also a sun pillar _and_ a small rainbow around the sun in the picture too?

Crepuscular Rays

When the clouds are thick, but the sun breaks through holes between them just enough to see rays of sun coming down, you are seeing Crepuscular rays! They can be very pretty.

Virga

Virga is rain that falls from the clouds, but you probably never even know it! How does this happen? Sometimes the air is so dry that the rain evaporates before it ever reaches the ground! Quite often you can see it hanging under the clouds, like in this picture.
Photo courtesy: University Corporation for Atmospheric Research

Thundersnow

Thundersnow is when there is thunder and lightning during a snow storm! Have you ever heard this before? In New England, it usually happens during a Nor'easter snow storm.
Photo courtesy: www.outventures.org

Ball Lightning

Ball lightning is something that not many people have seen. This may be the only picture ever taken of it because it happens so fast and you never know when it's coming. It is a ball of electricity that some people even say rolls around the ground or the floor! People who say they have seen it report it to be anywhere from the size of a pea to the size of a beach ball. Not much is known about ball lightning. One thing for sure, if you ever see ball lightning, don't try to play soccer with it!

Dust Devil

Dust devils look like little tornadoes but are very different. They don't happen near thunderstorms; in fact, they happen on sunny days! Sometimes when the wind starts to swirl around very quickly, a dust devil can form. Most of the time they are not dangerous, and aren't strong enough to injure anyone. Every once in a while, there is one strong enough to do damage to a house or hurt someone, but that is very rare.

Northern Lights

The Northern lights are a beautiful display of light in the night sky. The closer you are to the North Pole, the better the chance you have to see them. Sometimes you can see them here in New England if there are strong storms on the sun, known as sunspots. They are usually different shades of green, but can sometimes have other colors like red or yellow. They are also known as the *Aurora Borealis,* and happen from a combination of the sun and the magnetism in the Earth near the North Pole.

Fulgurites

Fulgurites are hollow tubes of glass - kind of like a silly straw made out of glass. What do they have to do with weather? They are formed when sand gets struck by lightning. If the temperature of the lightning is hot enough, it melts the sand into glass. Amazing!

Photo courtesy: www.minresco.com

I can see Mt. Washington from my house and school and I would like to know what those funny looking clouds that look like spaceships are. They are some· times above Mt. Washington.
Duncan McCorkhill,
Jefferson Elementary School, Jefferson, NH

These are very funny shaped clouds! Don't worry, many people see them and think they look like flying saucers or spaceships! Lenticular clouds form when wind blows over mountains and starts to swirl around in circles. This shapes the clouds in the same way that the wind is swirling around. You usually need to be somewhere near mountains, since lenticular clouds form near them. This picture was taken in Ossipee, NH.

Picture by Adam Judge

As you've seen in this book and in your life, the weather really does matter to everyone in the world! If you have plans for being outdoors, going to school, traveling, and almost everything else, you have to watch the weather.

We hope you now understand a little more about how the weather affects everything in your life, how different types of storms may cause different kinds of damage, and even how some types of weather happen!

Whenever you see some of the types of weather we've discussed, try talking to your family, friends, and teachers about it. They will be very surprised at how much you know about it now and even more surprised if you ask questions about the things you don't know. When the weather changes around you, pay attention to it because that's the first step in being a good weather observer! When the skies cloud up, watch if the clouds get darker and may be bringing rain. If you see lightning, count how long it takes to hear the thunder. When it's windy, ask an adult which direction it is coming from.

If you're interested in weather and think you might want to become a meteorologist when you grow up, pay attention in science and math class. Observe the weather all around you every day and watch how quickly it can change. For even more information on this or other things we've mentioned, after asking your parents, you can go to our website at **www.weatherfactsandfun.com.**